Grandfathers

by Lola M. Schaefer

Consulting Editor: Gail Saunders-Smith, Ph.D.
Consultant: Phyllis Edelbrock, First-Grade Teacher,
University Place School District, Washington

Pebble Books

an imprint of Capstone Press
Mankato, Minnesota

Pebble Books are published by Capstone Press
151 Good Counsel Drive, P.O. Box 669, Mankato, Minnesota 56002
http://www.capstone-press.com

2 3 4 5 6 7 07 06 05 04 03 02

Library of Congress Cataloging-in-Publication Data
Schaefer, Lola M., 1950–
    Grandfathers / by Lola M. Schaefer.
    p. cm.—(Families)
    Includes biographical references and index.
    Summary: Photographs and simple text describe grandfathers and some of the
things they do with their grandchilden.
    ISBN 0-7368-0257-6 (hardcover)
    ISBN 0-7368-8228-6 (paperback)
    1. Grandfathers—Juvenile literature. 2. Grandparent and child—Juvenile
literature. [1. Grandfathers.] I. Title. II. Series: Schaefer, Lola M., 1950– Families.
HQ759.9.S34   1999
306.874'5—dc21   98-46133

Note to Parents and Teachers

The Families series supports national social studies standards for
units related to identifying family members and their roles in the
family. This book describes and illustrates grandfathers and
activities they do with their grandchildren. The photographs
support emergent readers in understanding the text. The repetition
of words and phrases helps emergent readers learn new words.
This book also introduces emergent readers to subject-specific
vocabulary words, which are defined in the Words to Know section.
Emergent readers may need assistance to read some words and to
use the Table of Contents, Words to Know, Read More, Internet
Sites, and Index/Word List sections of the book.

Table of Contents

father

son

father

son

grandfather

grandson

Grandfathers are fathers
of mothers or fathers.

Some grandfathers
plant gardens.

Some grandfathers
shovel snow.

Some grandfathers
go for walks.

Some grandfathers
build toy boats.

Some grandfathers
play baseball.

Some grandfathers
read stories.

Some grandfathers
bake pies.

Grandfathers love
their grandchildren.

Words to Know

baseball—a game that two teams play with a bat and a ball; each team has nine players.

father—a male parent

garden—a place where people grow flowers, vegetables, shrubs, or other plants

grandchild—the child of a person's son or daughter

grandfather—the father of a person's mother or father

mother—a female parent

plant—to place a plant or seed in the ground so it can grow

shovel—to move things with a tool that has a long handle and a flat scoop

Read More

Bailey, Debbie. *Grandpa.* Toronto: Annick Press, 1994.

Baxter, Nicola. *Families.* Toppers. Chicago: Children's Press, 1996.

Nelson, JoAnne. *We Are Family.* Primarily Health. Bothell, Wash.: Wright Group, 1995.

Saunders-Smith, Gail. *Families.* People. Mankato, Minn.: Pebble Books, 1998.

Internet Sites

Family Fun
http://family.go.com

Grandparenting
http://www.thefamily.com/grandparenting

National Grandparent's Day
http://www.grandparents-day.com

Index/Word List

bake, 19
baseball, 15
build, 13
fathers, 5
gardens, 7
go, 11
grandchildren, 21
grandfathers, 5, 7, 9, 11,
   13, 15, 17, 19, 21
love, 21
mothers, 5

pies, 19
plant, 7
play, 15
read, 17
shovel, 9
snow, 9
stories, 17
their, 21
toy boats, 13
walks, 11

Word Count: 41
Early-Intervention Level: 6

Editorial Credits

Mari C. Schuh, editor; Steve Weil/Tandem Design, cover designer and illustrator;
   Kimberly Danger, photo researcher

Photo Credits

David F. Clobes, 1, 8, 16, 18
David F. Clobes Stock Photography/Chad D. Clobes 10
Diane Meyer, cover
International Stock/Patrick Ramsey, 12
Photo Network/Myrleen Ferguson Cate, 14
Unicorn Stock Photos/Chromosohm/Sohm, 20
Uniphoto, 4, 6

Special thanks to Joy Allison, Lori Hollenback, and Penny McCarthy, first-grade
teachers at Evergreen Primary in University Place, Washington, for reviewing the
books in the Families series.